Job Hunting Secrets for College Grads

By Shari Nomady and Yvette Brown

ISBN-13:
978-1511784863

ISBN-10:
1511784865

Meet the author.....

Over the last decade, I have leveraged my 30 years of marketing and sales expertise to successfully help my three daughters and countless friends land their first jobs out of college. My daughters didn't immediately see the opportunities that I did. Amazing internet tools like job title keyword searches and company and contact research to inexpensive business card printing and online portfolios were all available to give candidates who leveraged these tools the upper hand.

Unfortunately, a college degree didn't provide them with an understanding of how to use these resources to begin their career. That is the inspiration for this book: giving college grads a no-nonsense approach to finding and securing that first "real" job.

For the last 25 years, my business partner and I have been developing marketing programs for Fortune 500 companies and everyday name brands. We have delivered millions of incremental dollars to our clients by fusing proven strategies with emerging technologies.

The goal of our books is to democratize this quarter century of knowledge by sharing it to benefit the population at large.

To learn more about our company, X! PROMOS, Inc., visit www.xpromos.com

Table of Contents

Overview

Resources

Overview

Job hunting can be a daunting task. The world has suddenly gone from one where time is scheduled; assignments are clearly defined with expectations and deadlines, to one where no one really tells you what to do.

You've got a major, so you have some idea of what you're interested in, or good at. But perhaps you have no idea how that translates into a real job. Maybe you're a communications major. You've got a degree that claims you know how to communicate. But where do you go from there?

In the world of marketing and communications alone, there are a huge number of choices, from working on the "agency" side (in marketing, advertising, PR, digital, events, to name a few) to "client" side (in manufacturing, services, distribution, government, nonprofits and more).

Since it's your first job, you may want to cast a wider net. Broaden your search and apply for positions that pique your interest and some that may not. Let your interviewer decide whether or not you "fit the culture"; they know better about the company they represent.

Consider that every "no" gets you closer to a "yes". Identify a takeaway from every interview, and you'll get better at the process. Perhaps you'll become more selective in your applications, or you'll develop better answers to questions.

Always remember that, like marketing and sales in general, job hunting is a numbers game. You've got to "fill the funnel" with opportunities so that you can covert those leads into job offers.

Finally, remember that your first job won't be your last job. It doesn't have to be perfect. It needs to meet the basic personal criteria that you've established to be good enough to start.
This book will help you lay out and execute a successful game plan that will help you find opportunities, get noticed to get interviews, and rise above other candidates.

Happy hunting!

Chapter 1
Social Media: Set up and Clean up

Setting up the tools you need

First, get a professional email. Like your firstname.lastname @gmail.com. (or Yahoo). It's time to let go of "foxyliz" or "Yankees fan" as your email handle. This will also help you focus your attention on the email address where you can check and track correspondence to and from potential employers. If you have a smartphone, you should add this email account so that you have remote access, and can keep up and quickly respond to any queries sent.

With your smartphone you can also customize your signature to include your phone number to make it even more convenient for prospective employers to make contact with you. Make sure your voicemail message is professionally appropriate in case you do get a call.

Get a LinkedIn account

If you do not have a **www.LinkedIn.com** account, get one. It's the world's largest professional network, with nearly 350 million users worldwide. This is something you will need. Use a nice professional-looking head shot for your profile picture. Develop your profile with a background statement about yourself, along with all your "experience" (More on this in Chapter 2).

You can visit **https://www.linkedin.com/in/studentsample** to see a sample of a student's LinkedIn page. View this sample and other related samples to get a sense of how to prepare your LinkedIn page to best reflect you.

Now that you have a LinkedIn profile, start connecting with people and joining groups. You should be joining groups that are relevant to your field. For example, if you are going to be in the banking or accounting industry, then join those relevant groups. Search "accountants" or "banking" on LinkedIn and you will find 1,000's. Review them, and select a few. Look for ones that are active by taking note of the dates of the latest posts. This is your place to do your "business socializing". Many groups require you to "ask" to join; don't be wary. If your profile is relevant, you'll have no issue.

After you've joined the groups, get active by engaging with posts. You can do this by commenting on areas of interest, or by posting relevant articles you've found in the news. By searching on a term like "banking" in google news, or twitter, you'll come across recent developments that you could share via LinkedIn, with a comment or question posed to the group.

Go ahead and join a few groups that are relevant to your personal interests or hobbies. You never know how and where you will meet someone that can help you land your next job. Remember to join your college or University alumni groups. Add these too, as well as other groups related to your background (such as Greek organizations, volunteer organizations, etc.)

Add a website or portfolio
Depending on your background and/or area of interest, it may be relevant to create a website where you can show more about who you are. If you've got interest in a creative field, this can be the place where you show a portfolio of your work, or a link to your YouTube videos, or your blog.

If you're a reasonably good writer and have an opinion to share, consider setting up a blog. This will start to set you apart as an expert in your field. Now you can add that your resume and your LinkedIn profile.

Setting up a website (even with a blog) is easy and simple. You can search for website builders, or consider popular choices such as **Weebly, WIX, web.com**, or **Squarespace**. If you're not a designer by trade, take advantage of website building tools to make it simple and clean, and ideally create a look consistent with the rest of the "you" marketing materials.

Cleaning up your social stream

Next, make sure your Facebook, Instagram, Twitter and any other social media messages are CLEAN! I know you're thinking you don't have anything to worry about because your parents have been telling you this for years now and you've "been careful" about what you post. But, have your friends been careful? Did they "tag" you? These posts can also become public, especially if just one "friend" has an open Facebook account.

Before any more damage can be done, clean it up, lock it down and restrict tagging. Now is the time to make your accounts private and don't let people in you cannot trust. Delete all those posts and photos that are not suitable for the professional world. These types of posts include anything that shows or mentions racism, lewd or reckless behavior, drug use, excessive alcohol consumption, full or partial nudity, vandalism, or any other destructive or illegal activities.

This might be hard for you if you've been living in the "he who has the most "friends" wins world. The adult world is no longer about who has the "most" friends, instead it is about who has the "best contacts".

Moving forward, especially during the hiring phase, keeping it private might not be enough. There are some employers who will ask for access to your social media for review. It's not good enough to just be private; it needs to be clean and private. My daughter was on an interview where they asked her to sign into her Facebook account right then so they could see it on the spot!

Still not convinced? Google your name. What comes up? If you don't like the images or the links, do something about it. Chances are if you are a finalist in the interviewing process, the hiring manager will do this and it could make or break it for you in getting the offer. In fact, some HR managers in our independent survey admitted that a candidate's Facebook page prevented them from getting a job offer. It does happen.

Chapter 2
Preparing an attention-grabbing resume and cover letter

Preparing your resume

Aside from your digital profile, your resume and cover letter is the first direct opportunity for you to stand out from the competition. There are lots of resume templates out there that can take your resume from standard to outstanding. Check out **https://www.resumehelp.com**, **www.easyperfectresume.com**, **www.myperfectresume.com**.

Personally, I am a fan of the ones that include a graphic element and photo of you. This should be a photo that lets your personality shine through a bit. Not, I repeat, not a photo of you out with friends having drinks. This could be a nice shot of your walking your dog, at a park, or at the beach, or engaging in a favorite activity. Make sure you are dressed in casual clothes, but that does not include your swimsuit. Pick or plan to take a shot that fits nicely in the space (typically horizontal). Crop the photo so that you can see your face and also get a sense of the activity you're engaged in. If possible, take the photo with a SLR camera that has a better quality photo than your smartphone.

Resumes need to be concise, yet show quickly why you are a good candidate. The purpose is for it to pique the interviewer's interest in you, so that they want to see more. You also need a cover letter that grabs attention. That (and assuming the qualifications are met) will get you the interview. Many times, they don't read the entire resume until right before your interview – or they don't read it in detail. Never assume that the interviewer knows your resume as well as you.

If you're wondering why hiring managers are not reading every resume, let's do the math on that. If they received 200 resumes for EACH position they are hiring for, and they spent 20 seconds per resume that would take them over an hour for one position. There simply are not enough hours in the day to read everything on every resume that comes across their desk.

At a glance they are looking for: did they graduate from a major University, have good grades; were they involved in some activity and did they demonstrate leadership in this activity; did they have an internship or summer experience relatable to the job they are seeking? Beyond that, they are looking for something unique that breaks through the mundane clutter of the rest of the resumes on their desk.

Assuming this is your first "real" job out of college, you need an introductory statement about yourself. This statement should include something about your potential as an employee. Maybe you were a student athlete, in student government, or maybe you funded your own education, maybe you had an internship. All of these things start to give you workforce credibility.

For example, imagine an intro that read like this:
I am a former Division I college athlete looking to begin a career in sales/marketing where I can apply my acquired skillset developed from a lifetime of competitive team sports.

Playing competitive soccer since age 5 has prepared me well for a career, by learning many valuable life lessons, including the importance of preparation, cooperation, teamwork, leadership and a commitment to goals. I excelled as team captain because I have skillfully learned to direct a variety of personalities toward the team-focused goal for the day. I was also the connection between the players, the coaches and the athletic director, so I am comfortable dealing with all levels of management within an organization.

You can see how you can start to set yourself up for success and stand out from all the other basic resumes. It uniquely leverages this person's developed life skills in a way that is different from most other resumes.

Covering the basics

Your resume does need to include the basic facts: your education, major and dates; experience, with a brief description, dates and stand out accomplishments. Try to think about tangible accomplishments, such as raising $10,000 for a charity, or even being a part of a team that went to nationals.

Make sure your resume has your name, phone number and email address on it. Your resume should be one page at this point. Include any skills you have, such as with computer software like: Microsoft Office, Adobe, etc. Don't overlook special skills you may have developed or learned that are in high demand, like Google Analytics, Facebook ads, or mobile app development.

Make sure you have at least one impressive reference. They might not check it, but having one adds to your credibility. This could be a professor, a coach or someone in the business world who has known you for a long time.

Writing your cover letter

Now that you have the resume, write a brief cover letter. This is important because most of the jobs you apply for will be on line and the cover letter will give you an edge, if it's short and to the point. Since you may be applying for a few different types of jobs (sales, marketing, banking, accounting, production, post production, etc.), you will want to customize the first paragraph to fit each job you are applying for. Customizing letters sounds tedious and time consuming (it is) but it is a KEY INGREDIENT to standing out. It's one step to show WHY YOU SHOULD BE CONSIDERED. You must always think about the process from the perspective of the COMPANY that's looking to make a financial commitment to YOU.

The balance of the cover letter can be more of a template. Think of it in four sections:

> **1.** Customized intro paragraph – how your experience matches what they are looking for. Make sure you mention the company name.
> **2.** Tell them why you are applying for THEIR job.

3. Some details about the type of person they can expect to have on their team if they hire you. Be specific here. Everyone is an eager team-player.

4. Close with how you're looking forward to hearing more about the opportunity and meeting them. Mention the company name again.

Additional considerations for your cover letter:

1. Don't forget to include your phone number and email on both the cover letter and the resume.

2. If they asked for a salary requirement – Answer this or you will not be considered.

3. If you are applying for a job in a town you do not live in, explain why or they will not consider you.

Look the part

Spend $30 to get business cards made. Make sure they match the resume and cover letter. The typestyle should be the same on all three. There should be an overall graphic theme to all three pieces. The cards should have the following on them: Name, phone number, email address and a title. For example, if you are looking for a job in marketing it might read "Marketing Specialist". Here are some links to order business cards: **www.vistaprint.com**, **www.overnightprints.com**, **www.zazzle.com**.

Bring three copies of your resume and a stack of business cards to EVERY interview. You never know when you will need to provide the resume to someone who forgot to print it or bring it to the conference room. ALWAYS BE PREPARED. Make sure you hand each interviewer a business card at the beginning of the meeting. They should give you one of theirs and if they don't, ask for one. This will be helpful for your follow up. Now, you're ready to start the search.

Chapter 3
Creating a system to search

Informational Meetings and Interviews
Now that you have cleaned up your social media, set up your LinkedIn profile and you have a resume and business cards, start talking to people. This means, ask your parents, parents' friends and their friends if they know anyone in your related field that would be willing to take an "informational meeting" with you. These are good for networking and fact finding. This will get you and your resume out there and give your practice meeting with people.

The purpose of these meetings is for you to ask questions that will help you in your job search. Do not ask them what positions they have available at their company for you. More appropriate questions would be, how did you get into this field? What suggestions do you have for some looking to get into this field today? What options do you see for someone in this field? Of course, they will ask some questions about you and if they know anyone looking, they will pass your information along. These types of meetings don't typically lead to jobs, but they help with your networking and you will learn things that will make you a better candidate during your search.

Posting your resume and establishing your search system.
The first place to go to is LinkedIn. You have a profile there and they have a "jobs" section. As with most job sites, you can search by key words and by zip code. When searching by keywords, you can use the industry you are seeking and you can add the words "entry level" to the beginning of that key word. Keep refining the key words until you have exhausted the open jobs. Keep in mind that different organizations use different terms for the same job. At first, make your search terms broad to see the possibilities, and then narrow the search as you get a better handle on what appeals to you. Make note of the best key words—you'll need them for other searches.
Stay clear of the "scam" jobs. Three things to remember here:
1. If it sounds too good to be true, it is.
2. If the interview meeting place seems shady when you arrive, trust your instinct and don't go in.
3. If you get there and your intuition is telling you this is not right, leave.

There are a lot of places out there that look to hire people for "events" or "event marketing" that are a bit sketchy. STAY CLEAR. If someone calls you for an interview and you are not familiar with the company, then Google them. If you do not like what you are reading about them, cancel the interview.

Posting your resume online
There are many places on line to post your resume and search for jobs. Check out these for starters:

www.indeed.com

www.zillionresumes.com

www.monster.com

www.careerbuilder.com

You may find other sites that you like; do some research and start posting it.

Although this step won't hurt your process, do not assume companies will find you once you post your resume. These sites are mostly for recruiters use. You will still need to be actively looking for a job. As I told all my kids, if you do not have a job today, your full time job is to find a job!

Other places to look for job opportunities
If there are specific companies you're interested in working at, make sure you visit their corporate website directly and look for career opportunities. You can also check out trade publications in key industries, and even check social media like Twitter, as some companies post via social media.

Your search system
The first thing you need to do is establish your system for the search. Here is what I have told candidates to do. Feel free to modify this, but this is a good place to start.

1. Make a tracking sheet. This sheet will be an Excel-type chart that has the following information:

> Company Name
> Position
> Contact Name
> Contact email
> Phone Number
> Date you Applied
> Source of Job Listing
> Follow Up

You can track electronically or by hand. You can also download a free PDF or Excel template at www.xpromos1.com/xpert-training.
You will need to be organized so when someone calls or emails and says I would like to set up an interview, you can go back and re read what the job post was. It also helps you to not apply to the same job twice. And lastly, it tracks your work so you can see that you are staying on pace. To track where you saw the post, either print out the job so you have the source and the job description, or book mark it or use a tool like **www.dropbox.com** to manage all the jobs you have applied for.

2. Apply for 30-40 jobs per week *minimum*. In the beginning, there will be more out there because you are just getting started. This is a reasonable goal and can be achieved. If you are not doing this, you are lowering your odds of getting a job. Remember, this is a numbers game, and you need to apply to a large number of positions to increase the number of interviews you get.

3. Follow up if there is a contact name or an email. Call and/or email them in a week stating your continued interest and checking in on their progress.

4. Carry those business cards everywhere and talk to people and tell them you are looking for a job. Make sure the business card has your LinkedIn address and twitter if you are using this. I recommend that you have a twitter account and post things relevant to your industry and start tweeting back and forth with others in your industry to establish credibility and increase your personal brand. If you are seeking a job in a very creative/artsy industry I highly recommend you have an Instagram account and/or YouTube channel where you can showcase some of your work.

Once you get going in your search system, you will find that you are tracking leads at varying levels in your "job funnel". You always need to spend time continuing to fill the funnel with new opportunities (new positions come available daily), while also applying for new positions, following up on applications, and following up on second and third interviews.

One of the biggest mistakes made is slowing down after a good interview. Remember that nothing is done until it's signed and delivered. Even if an interviewer says they want to make you an offer, many things can prevent that from happening. Maybe the company loses a major piece of business they expected to win, or maybe your contact leaves. It's even possible that the offer that comes in is substantially different than what you expected. The point is, never stop filling the funnel and searching until you've officially landed the job that meets your needs.

Chapter 4
Formulating your Elevator Pitch

You are now ready for the personal elevator pitch.

This is something that you must be able to recite at any moment without hesitation and without sounding like it's "memorized". This is why it takes practice.

This will be used every day, every time someone says, "what's your story" or "what are you up to now". Or use it as an intro at social events, and business-networking events. It has to be succinct (less time than it takes for a typical elevator ride).

The heart of the pitch

In three sentences, tell me something unique about yourself, what you are looking for and why you will be good at it.

Everyone's pitch will change and evolve with time and experience. Developing your first one is the hardest.

Here is an example of one of mine. People ask me all the time "What do you do"?

X! Promos is an independent marketing firm with over 25 years of experience driving sales for Fortune 500 companies and everyday name brands. We do this by fusing proven strategies with evolving technologies to create programs with impactful results. Typically clients come to us when they are frustrated with their own internal marketing efforts, concerned about increased competition in the market place or preparing to launch a new product or service. Do you know anyone who could use these services?

If it's appropriate, end your pitch with a question.

Once you have your pitch written down, practice saying it in front of a mirror. Reading it is NOT the same as saying it out loud. When you speak it out loud you will discover the part(s) that don't sound natural: you stumble over and just can't say with a natural cadence. If more practicing doesn't clear it up, then it's time to edit the pitch. When you've got it sounding right, practice on people you know who can give you honest feedback on how you sound. Once you're comfortable with it, be ready to use it at a moment's notice.

Chapter 5
Nailing your interview

The First Interview: Understand the Objective
The first interview is really a meet and greet. It's a chance for you to see the company, meet some people and get a vibe and overall first impression of this potential employer. Remember, you can't change the first impression of one another.

30 Seconds to make your first impression
Your system is working and you have the interview and you've done your research on the company and you are feeling prepared. Do not blow it on the 30 second first impression.

Make sure you are dressed appropriately. You can never be too overdressed. Even if you know it's a very casual work environment and your interview is on a Friday, do not make the mistake of showing up too casual. When in doubt, wear a suit and you can always take the jacket off during the interview.

Next, make sure you are on time. NO EXCUSES! Plan to arrive 5-10 minutes early. Allow extra time for traffic. Walk in 10 minutes early, sit your car and prepare if you've arrived more than 10 minutes early. Do NOT bring in your Starbucks, food or anything. You will only be here for an hour. You should only walk in with a folder with your resumes, a pad of paper for taking notes and a pen. A purse is acceptable. If you must bring your phone in, turn it off and keep it in your purse or pocket. DO NOT have it out even waiting in the lobby. Remember, you are deciding if this is a good fit for you too. If you are on your phone, you are missing a lot of interaction just sitting and observing.

Next, make sure you greet the front office person with a smile and be polite and kind. Many times, the hiring manager will ask them what their impression was of the candidates. When you walk in, hand them one of your business cards and say, "Hi, I am XYZ, I'm here for my 2:00 appointment with _____."

Lastly, make sure you greet them with a smile, direct eye contact and a firm handshake. This does not need to be a hand-breaking grip, but no wet fish handshakes.

That's it. You're 30 seconds are up and you either passed or failed. Make it count.

Is this a good fit?
The objective of this first interview is for both you and the company to decide if you want to move on to another interview for more details. Try to take note of the office environment and personal items of your interviewers. This could help you strike up a conversation during this interview, or during follow-up conversations.

Questions for you to ask
Make sure you have questions prepared for the person you are interviewing with also. Here is a list of a few questions you can choose from to keep in your arsenal:

1. Prior to the first interview, Google the company. Go to their website and checkout their social media posts to find something you can comment about. For instance, maybe they just received an award or honor for something in the community or their industry – comment on this – ask about it. The idea is to let them know you did your homework, and you are genuinely interested in working for them. Maybe they have launched a new product or service that you are familiar with – talk about it.
2. What does a typical day look like in this position?
3. What's the number one quality you are looking for in the candidate you will hire?
4. Why is this job open today?
5. If you could wave a magic wand and create the perfect candidate for the job what would I have in common with that person?
6. How can I make an immediate impact on the department or company?
7. How would I spend for my first 30-60 day on the job?
8. What's the best and worst thing that's happened to the company in the last year?
9. Tell me a bit more about your background and work history.
10. What drives you crazy?

11. Why did you decide to work for this company?
12. How can I make you look like a hero to your boss?
13. What's most important to your boss?
14. What 3 adjectives would your co-workers use to describe you?
15. If you hired me, what would I need to do in the first year for you to say this was the best hiring decision I ever made?

DO NOT TALK ABOUT SALARY OR BENEFITS at this first interview. It is rare, but if **they** bring it up, then it's okay to talk about it.

During your first interview, **ask about their hiring process**. This will help you understand how things will work and when it's appropriate for more follow up if you haven't heard about your next step. A typical process might sound like this:

 "We will be notifying all the candidates in the next two weeks if they will be returning for a second round of interviews. We expect the final decision to be made three weeks after the second round." If they don't tell you specifically when to expect to hear back from them, ASK! Otherwise, you don't seem interested, and you don't know when it's appropriate to follow up again.

Commonly asked interview questions
Our survey of Hiring Managers tells us you can expect these questions during the interview process. So, study them, prepare an answer for each of them. Just like the elevator pitch, practice them out loud and in front of a mirror.

Side bar note here: I practiced this with my youngest daughter. We made sure she was very comfortable with the answers. After she was hired they were talking in the office one day about the interviewing process. One of the managers said the biggest reason she was hired over the other final candidate was her answer to the question "Tell us about yourself". Apparently, the other candidate had a long rambling answer that went nowhere. My daughter had a very concise and direct answer that weaved in a little personal and some business to it. The one manager said she knew as soon as she answered that question she would be hired! So, it pays to do the work and make sure you have done the practice. Practice with a working adult that you are comfortable with and respect. Ideally, someone in your field, but this is not a must. What's most important is that you practice with an adult who will help you.

Here are the most commonly asked questions at an interview:

1. Tell me about yourself.

2. Tell me about your weaknesses.

3. Why did you leave your last job? (Be careful when answering this question. Do not trash talk on the company or reveal company secrets.) This will be a testament to your character, the person they are looking to hire. In fact, several of our surveyed Hiring Managers indicated that bad-mouthing a former employer was the biggest mistake a candidate could make.

4. Why should we hire you?

I was coaching someone during her search for a new job and the interviewing process. We talked about how sometimes they will have one last question for you and it is "Why should we hire you?" I told her that if the interview went well and she felt a good connection with them to consider answering that with "Why wouldn't you hire me?" We practiced this a lot. You can pull it off if you can say it without being cocky. She did it and she got the job. Ten years later, the head of HR at this multi-billion dollar company still talks about how that was the best answer to that question ever!

Phone, Skype or Face to Face

Your first interview could be via phone, Skype, or face to face. Many times an employer will start with phone interviews in an effort to save time. Hiring managers can tell within 5-10 minutes over the phone if this is someone who they will bring in for a face to face interview. Skype is often used for the same reason, and used when you are interviewing for a job that is not near you.

When preparing for the phone interview, make sure you are in a quiet place, where there will be no distractions. Remember, this is an interview and you need to think of it as being in their office. Therefore, do not take other calls, do not text during the call and certainly, do not put yourself in a situation where there will be distractions. If you are going to use your cell phone, test the area with a friend and make sure there is reception. Get to the location 5 minutes before your call and be ready. Since this is over the phone, have a note card with all the points you want to make sure you cover. This would include questions to ask them, points you want to communicate about your experience and something noteworthy you know about the company.

If your first interview is going to be via Skype, make sure you have done the following things to ensure success.

1. Confirm the hiring manager's Skype user name and make sure you add that person to your contacts so you can easily connect on Skype.

2. Confirm who is calling who and at what time.

3. Make sure you are in an area that is very clean with a generic background. If there is a window behind you, close the curtain so they can see you. Do not have a messy area with lots of things around you or else the person will be busy looking at these things and not paying attention to what you are saying.

4. Test the area and your Skype with a friend before your call. Make sure you are comfortable using Skype. They will be looking at how you respond and react to questions.

5. Lastly, you can have a note card on this call. Just have it in front of you where you can look at it, but it's not in view of the interviewer.

Understand Your Odds
I know it sounds daunting when they say we received over 200 resumes and we are interviewing 30 candidates and we've selected you for an interview.

Why do they need to set up 30 interviews? Let me break it down.

> 20% will not show up
> 20% will decide not to interview because they got a job, changed their plans, etc.
> 20% will show up late
> 20% will show up ill-prepared or dress inappropriately
> 20% will show up early, prepared and dressed appropriately

Will you be one of the 6 in the final running for the job? If so, make sure you make a great first impression, and make the interview count with all your preparation.

Chapter 6
What to do after the interview

Saying Thank You

You must send a thank you email to everyone you met at the first interview within 24 hours; ideally as soon as you return to your computer or digital device. Hopefully you got everyone's business card and you can send a personal follow up thanking them for their time and interest. Make sure you reference something in the email about the interview. For example, "I was thinking more about your comment on XYZ and I have a few more thoughts on that now".

These thank you emails and follow up emails should be brief and to the point.

The first paragraph should be simple: "Thank you for taking the time to meet with me about the XYZ position. I enjoyed learning about it and I'm most excited about the _____ part of the position because _____."

The second paragraph should state some sort of reference to the interview. It could be something as simple as "I saw that your team won or traded someone...." If you noticed something in the office that tied them to a sports team for example.

The last paragraph should reference a follow up: "When can I expect to hear about the next step? I look forward to hearing from you soon."

Make sure you have an email sign off complete with your full name, phone number and email address.

Sometimes hiring managers use this as a test to one, determine if you really are interested in working for them, and two, see your follow up skills. After all, if this position requires any follow up skills (and nearly every job does) then they want to test that out before they hire.

Take The Thank You Note One Step Further:
If this is the IDEAL job for you and you really want this job, I suggest you hand deliver something the following day. (This does not REPLACE the thank you email; it is in addition to it.) If you are interviewing for a job at an accounting firm, you could deliver a very nice "Tax Survival Bag" of "treats". Do something very clever that ties to them. One of my daughters interviewed at a very dog-friendly company and the person she interviewed with had his dog there that day. She went to a pet store and got a handful of the "homemade" dog treats and put them in a box with a message about her level of service, since she was interviewing for a job that related to service.

The Follow Up
ALWAYS follow up – you are not being a pest, you are in the real working world and this is a requirement.

During the first interview, you asked about their process. Hopefully, you went home and made note of that on your tracking sheet. Now you know when to follow up with a phone call and/or email that asks about the next step. Maybe the next step is an interview with the department head and that was supposed to be scheduled in 2 weeks. However, maybe something came up and they are not available that week and it's been pushed back a week. A hiring manager will appreciate that you took note and you had the skill set to follow up and inquire. According to our survey of hiring managers, typically candidates can expect to have up to three interviews for an entry-level position. The average time it takes for a company to fill an entry level position is 3-5 weeks.

Continue to follow up until you get closure on the opportunity. You invested your time in the interview and the company should respect you enough to provide an answer on the status of the job you interviewed for.

Feedback from Hiring Managers

We asked Hiring Managers "What's the biggest mistake entry level candidates make on his/her resume?" The most common answer was: "Not telling the truth". Did you graduate? They will answer "Yes". Then after the company checks they discover that they didn't pay their tuition or fines and therefore, *technically,* did not graduate. If the company has asked the question, then it's important to them. They will fact check. Don't lie.

Our survey also discovered that another mistake candidates make during the interviewing process is not adequately selling themselves. Interviewing is like shopping. The person doing the interview needs to want to "BUY" this product (YOU)! Don't sell yourself short. Make sure you sell your own key attributes.

When we asked the Hiring Managers what piece of advice you would give a new college graduate looking for their job, we found some insightful answers. Don't ask for a million dollars. Just because salary.com says XYZ position 'can' make up to $85,000, does not mean that every employer can or will pay that. There are several factors that go into a salary. It is advantageous for candidates to research the area or leave the question "open" for negotiations.

"Be patient, do your homework". Do not jump into a job because of a higher salary. Look into the entire total compensation package. An employer that flashes around a large amount of money may be hiding behind it.

Chapter 7
You got the job! Now what?

Start your search for your mentor and start your networking.

Everyone needs a mentor. This may be someone you work with; it may be someone in the business world that you trust to help you. But find someone that you can go to and ask questions and get advice from. Someday, you will return the favor and be a mentor to someone.

Now it's also time to begin the networking. First, "Link In" with people you are working with, people you meet in business, vendors, competitors, sales people, etc. Go to networking events and bring your business card and practice your new elevator pitch. (You will need a new one now that you have a job!)

Next, keep that LinkedIn profile updated. Keep adding milestones to the profile. If you receive an award or achievement recognition, post that! One of my daughters was called by CBS Entertainment to interview based on her LinkedIn profile. Recruiters and Hiring Managers look here for candidates!

I met someone who told me they spent every Monday "networking". They called or emailed 25% of their contacts every Monday. That way they made direct contact with everyone in their network at least monthly! Now that's someone who's working their system!

Good luck!

Resources

If you still feel you need a little more TLC with your search, you can reach me at **snomady@xpromos.com** for personal consulting.

We offer a personal service package to help candidates speed up and improve their odds of getting a job offer. Visit our website at: **www.xpromos1.com/xpert-training** for more details.

Looking to have someone speak on this topic at your next workshop or career event? Contact me at **snomady@xpromos.com.**